RYAN McGINNESS

MINDSCAPES

520 West 21st Street
New York NY 10011

tel +1 212 445 0051
www.milesmcenery.com

525 West 22nd Street
New York NY 10011

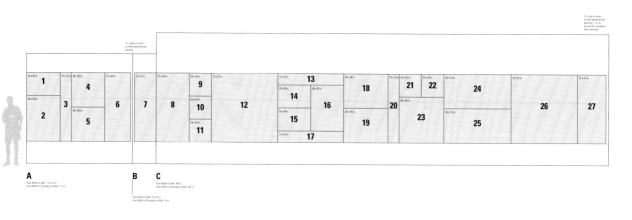

A
Total Width of Wall: 114 1/4 in.
Total Width of Paintings on Wall: 112 in.

B
Total Width of Wall: 25 3/4 in.
Total Width of Paintings on Wall: 24 in.

C
Total Width of Wall: 490 in.
Total Width of Paintings on Wall: 487 in.

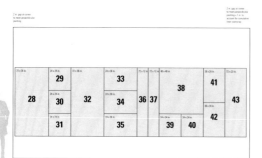

D
Total Width of Wall: 256 1/2 in.
Total Width of Paintings on Wall: 251 in.

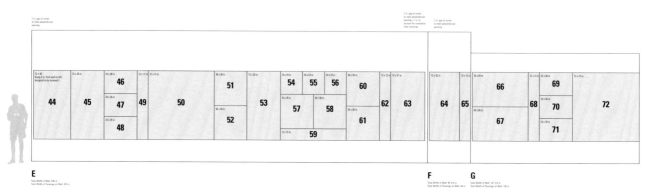

E
Total Width of Wall: 430 in.
Total Width of Paintings on Wall: 425 in.

F
Total Width of Wall: 45 3/4 in.
Total Width of Paintings on Wall: 44 in.

G
Total Width of Wall: 181 3/4 in.
Total Width of Paintings on Wall: 180 in.

Scale

1 ft. (x1)   1 in. (x12)

As one painting:
Mindscapes, 2020, acrylic on linen over 72 panels of various sizes, 6' x 126'11" total

RYAN McGINNESS AND HIS
MICRO-MACRO CANVAS MURAL

By Jori Finkel

The Renaissance artists who popularized the tradition of painting on canvas were, to different degrees, growing tired of what we today call site-specificity. They were seeking freedom from the altarpieces that held their artworks in one place, as well as from church patronage, which fixed the works into one hermeneutic system. They were looking for ways to circulate their paintings, which were increasingly replacing religious narratives with secular genres like landscapes, portraits, and still lifes. They wanted something as easy to transport as books and, ideally, as easy to trade as currency.

So while European painting was in the process of relinquishing its religious roots and becoming more secular, it also relinquished its grip on architecture and became more portable. Take Rembrandt, who began making portraits on canvas in the 1630s,[1] a time of great urbanization and commercialization in Amsterdam that was marked by the rise of the merchant class (and, not coincidentally, the boom and bust of tulip mania). Rembrandt's easel paintings, inventoried most thoroughly in 1656 because of his bankruptcy proceedings,[2] ultimately became chips in the blue-chip Old Masters market, traveling widely to make their homes in public and private collections across many different countries.

This tension between site-specificity and canvas painting remains strong today, as the two typically remain on opposite sides of the value coin. But with his new *Mindscapes* exhibition at Miles McEnery Gallery, Ryan McGinness has figured out how to have it both ways. He has created an artwork that is dramatically and thoroughly site-specific but is, at the same time, highly portable and marketable. He has found a way to have his mural cake and eat it—or slice it up for collectors—too.

To divulge the basic recipe, he has created a painting of paintings, arranging 72 different canvases that share some common motifs and colors into one

Layout for *Mindscapes* Exhibition, 2019, digital file

Sir John Gilbert RA, *Rembrandt painting a portrait*, 1860 © Royal Academy of Arts, London

composition. While the canvases themselves come in nine different sizes (the most popular being 2-by-3 feet), he has hung them flush up against each other so that, viewed from a distance, they appear to be one large artwork, 6 feet tall and nearly 127 feet long, wrapping around all the walls of the gallery except the front. (The measurement of 127 feet was dictated by the gallery layout, 6 feet is the artist's height, and 72 came from the year of his birth, 1972.) Seen from across West 21st Street through the gallery's glass doors and façade, or from right inside the gallery entrance, the work has the punch of a single mural.

The overall effect is art on the scale of architecture, creating the feeling of a grand public-lobby mural or chateau-scaled tapestry. But the individual canvas components can later be exhibited alone or reconfigured into smaller groups, whether diptychs or groups of three or four pieces. The gallery-sized canvas puzzle can be taken apart in numerous ways.

"I haven't had a gallery show in New York in five years, so I wanted to do something challenging," the artist said during a studio visit. "I wanted to make a bold statement, while also recognizing this is a gallery that has to be able to sell each painting."[3]

The paintings feature a baroque profusion of images pulled from McGinness's vast symbol system: an extensive inventory of his own drawings organized

Hieronymus Bosch, *The Garden of Earthly Delights*, circa 1490–1510. Courtesy Museo Nacional del Prado, Madrid

into various categories, including figures, hands, flowers and studio tools, plus an umbrella category known as "mindscapes" for more psychedelic-inspired concoctions. He calls this system "a periodic table" and regularly combines the stylized drawings, or "elements," with each other to create what he calls "compounds." Expect to spot as well some familiar bits of art history, visual references to works by Marcel Duchamp, Pablo Picasso and Hans Arp—Dada is a favorite movement—making cameos here and there.

Given the density of this imagery, which recalls some hyperactive styles of street art as well as overloaded Pattern and Decoration painting, the work rewards both stepping back for the panoramic view and zeroing in on small details or tableaux. Or shifting from one vantage point to another, a process that McGinness describes experiencing when looking at the phantasmagorical paintings of Hieronymus Bosch.

"I love how *The Garden of Earthly Delights* is high-impact from afar but also so rewarding when you get close and investigate—you get lost in that world of details," he said. "Not all paintings are rewarding when you look closely." He later added, "I like a wide range of scale shifts within the same picture plane as a way to force different viewing distances."[4]

The single biggest perspectival shift at play in this "Mindscapes" exhibition, from viewing the artwork as a single piece to seeing its component parts, is

#metadata, 2016, installation view, Kohn Gallery, Los Angeles
Courtesy Kohn Gallery © 2020 Ryan McGinness Studios, Inc /
Artist Rights Society (ARS), New York

an unusual move for McGinness but it's not entirely unfamiliar, as he has a history of treating his paintings as building blocks that can be arranged in different permutations and combinations.

On two occasions, starting with a show at the Kohn Gallery in Los Angeles in 2016 called *#metadata*, he has bolted together used silkscreen frames to build gallery mazes that visitors can enter and navigate.

And he has cleverly arranged canvases into mural-like formations in a few of his earlier exhibitions. Most notably, in 2017, he wrapped the perimeter of a gallery at the Cranbrook Art Museum in Bloomfield Hills, Michigan, with examples of his "Studio Views" paintings positioned side-by-side, so they appeared somewhat continuous. Fostering the illusion of continuity: At 7 feet tall, each painting was the same height and each featured, running along its bottom edge, a pattern representing a studio floor. Disrupting the illusion: Each painting's floorboard pattern had a different wood grain and color, and some canvases used different background colors for the studio walls as well.

Studio Views, 2017, installation view, Cranbrook Art Museum, Bloomfield Hills
Photo by PD Rearick, Courtesy Cranbrook Art Museum © 2020 Ryan McGinness
Studios, Inc / Artist Rights Society (ARS), New York

Dream Garden, 2002, installation view, Deitch Projects
© 2020 Ryan McGinness Studios, Inc / Artist Rights Society
(ARS), New York

Greater New York, 2005, installation view, P. S.1
Contemporary Art Center © 2020 Ryan McGinness
Studios, Inc / Artist Rights Society (ARS), New York

McGinness also has a long history of painting directly on walls, in both outdoor and indoor environments. The indoor environments include murals for Deitch Projects in 2002 and MoMA PS1's Greater New York show in 2005. For the Deitch show, "Dream Garden," a collaboration with Julia Chiang, he painted a landscape on the wall filled with flora and fauna—most memorably some shadowy trees that related to real landscaping transplanted into the gallery.

He has also used large vinyl sheets to cover walls in an industrial twist on the mural tradition. For a work called 53 Women, he created a 108-foot digitally printed vinyl mural lining the wall near a Citibank parking lot in La Jolla, California, in 2011. It consists of three large horizontal panels featuring an assortment of highly stylized female nudes in bright pinks, oranges, yellows, greens, and blues that make them appear like colorful children's stickers, nudity notwithstanding.

In 2016, when the Longchamp flagship store on the Rue Saint-Honoré in Paris was undergoing renovation, he wrapped the townhouse façade with his high-impact images in high-voltage colors. As Jean Cassegrain, Longchamp's chief executive, told the press at the time, "Renovations of this magnitude in such a conspicuous location need something spectacular that goes beyond a simple tarp."[5] Recently, he added: "The concept of having artisans patiently renovating the 18th-century stonework of the façade under Ryan's work was a great match to what our house stands for," describing a pairing of crafts-manship and innovation.[6]

Côté Maison writer Virginie Bertrand called McGinness's addition a "pop culture fresco" that is jam-packed with "icons, symbols, graphic figures and colorful swirls."[7]

You can make out within it details from his "black hole" or event-horizon images, Warhol-inspired hair wigs, a version of the Dadaist Raoul Hausmann's Mechanical Head, a psychedelic vision of a smile turning into dripping rainbow hair, an ouroboros, a ziggurat pyramid and an image of businessmen eating from the same tree. There are also a few stretches with negative space, a visual respite in the urban cacophony—something that he is also offering to punctuate his Miles McEnery Gallery mural.

Longchamp Building Wrap, Paris
Mindscapes, 2016, digitally printed vinyl stretched over building facade
Courtesy Longchamp, Paris © 2020 Ryan McGinness Studios, Inc / Artist Rights Society (ARS),
New York

The Longchamp "fresco" has a different look and feel than the new gallery
installation, though. The Paris mural was printed on vinyl in bright colors that
pop at night when illuminated by colored lights. Different sections were boxed
off visually with black borders, making for a fake mural cut into faux canvases
instead of a pseudo mural made out of real paintings. And the drama of seeing
these electric images play against the traditional Parisian architecture of the
1st arrondissement—the Longchamp building itself, from 1735, has landmark
status—was made for Instagram in ways that the New York gallery installation
is not.

For the gallery installation, all acrylic on canvas, McGinness clearly enjoyed the
process of screen painting and the chance to play up the particular qualities
of his medium. He creates texture by layering one screen-printed image over
another in spots. And, most dramatically, he has decided to use pearlescent
backgrounds, metal leafing and fluorescent colors throughout his canvases.
The resulting images are notoriously hard to reproduce.

Mindscape 12 (detail), 2019, acrylic and metal leaf on linen

"These foils and colors don't reproduce well in RBG or CMYK," he said, referring to the common color schemes used for digital and printed displays respectively. "You have to see these things in person."[8]

Undoubtedly, elements of the new gallery show will turn up here or there on social media. And I know my own impulse when facing an artwork this expansive and extensive is to take out my iPhone to see what it can see, an instinctive if not entirely rational attempt to bring an experience down to size. But in some ways, this mural is made for your full body, not just your eyes—proprioception as well as perception. Walking up to it, backing away from it and moving around it, you just might create a maze of your own making. ▪

Jori Finkel is a regular contributor from Los Angeles to *The New York Times* and *The Art Newspaper*. Her new book, *It Speaks to Me* (Prestel), features 50 leading artists on artworks that inspire them from museums across the world.

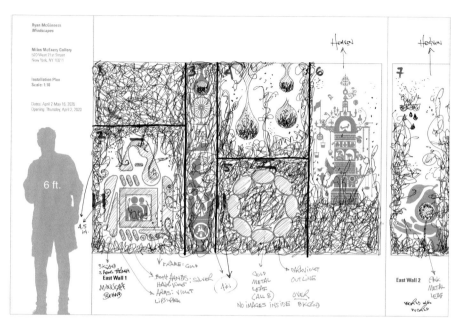

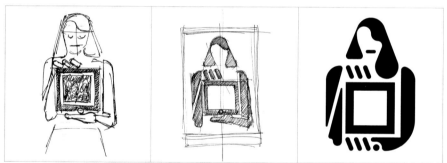

Above: *Sketch for exhibition paintings*, 2019, ink and toner on paper, 11 ½ x 18 inches (29.2 x 45.7 cm)
Below: *Sketch Process and Final Drawing*, 2019, ink on paper and digital vector file

Notes

1. Ernst Van de Wetering, "The Canvas Support," in *Rembrandt, The Painter at Work* (Berkeley and Los Angeles: University of California Press, 2009), 91.

2. Simon Schama, *Rembrandt's Eyes* (New York: Alfred A. Knopf, 1999), 612.

3. Ryan McGinness, interview by the writer with the artist in his Centre Street studio in New York, Oct. 24, 2019.

4. Ryan McGinness, interview by the writer with the artist in his Centre Street studio in New York, Oct. 24, 2019.

5. Bertrand, Virginie. "Longchamp se réinvente en collaboration avec l'art new-yorkais" ("Longchamp Reinvents Itself through a Collaboration with New York Art"), Côté Maison website, June 19, 2016.

6. Jean Cassegrain, email to the writer on Nov. 6, 2019.

7. Bertrand, Virginie, Ibid.

8. Ryan McGinness, interview by the writer with the artist in his Centre Street studio in New York, Oct. 24, 2019.

Various Drawings, 2015–2019, digital vector files

Various Drawings, 2015–2019, digital vector files

18

Various Drawings, 2015–2019, digital vector files

Mindscape 1, 2019
Acrylic on linen
24 x 36 inches
61 x 91.4 cm

30

Mindscape 2, 2019
Acrylic and metal leaf on linen
48 x 36 inches
121.9 x 91.4 cm

Mindscape 3, 2019
Acrylic and metal leaf on linen
72 x 12 inches
182.9 x 30.5 cm

Mindscape 4, 2019
Acrylic and metal leaf on linen
36 x 36 inches
91.4 x 91.4 cm

Mindscape 5, 2019
Acrylic and metal leaf on linen
36 x 36 inches
91.4 x 91.4 cm

38

Mindscape 6, 2019
Acrylic and metal leaf on linen
72 x 28 inches
182.9 x 71.1 cm

Mindscape 7, 2019
Acrylic and metal leaf on linen
72 x 24 inches
182.9 x 61 cm

Mindscape 8, 2019
Acrylic and metal leaf on linen
72 x 36 inches
182.9 x 91.4 cm

Mindscape 9, 2019
Acrylic and metal leaf on linen
24 x 24 inches
61 x 61 cm

Mindscape 10, 2019
Acrylic on linen
24 x 24 inches
61 x 61 cm

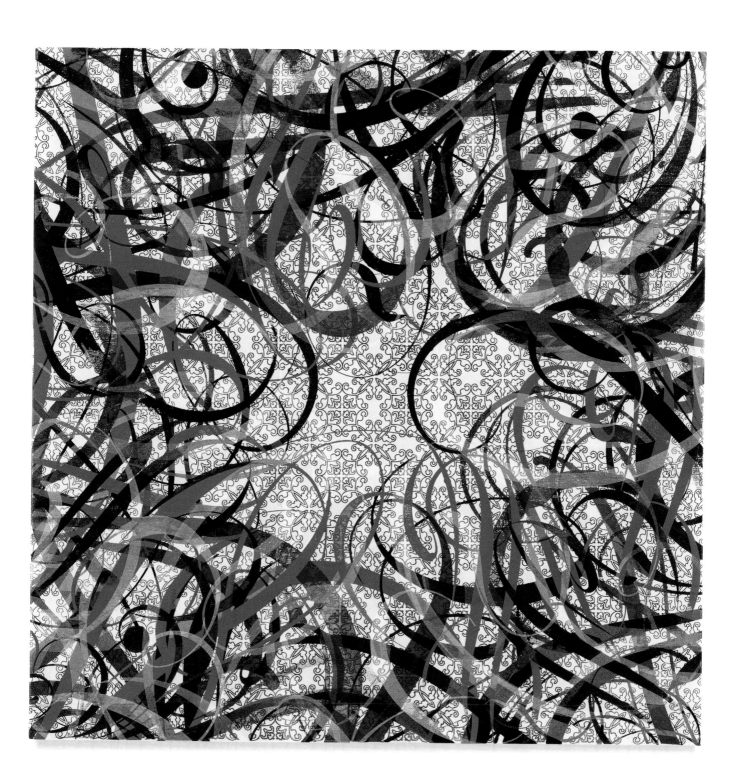

48

Mindscape 11, 2019
Acrylic on linen
24 x 24 inches
61 x 61 cm

Mindscape 12, 2019
Acrylic and metal leaf on linen
72 x 72 inches
182.9 x 182.9 cm

Mindscape 13, 2019
Acrylic on linen
12 x 72 inches
30.5 x 182.9 cm

Mindscape 14, 2019
Acrylic and metal leaf on linen
24 x 36 inches
61 x 91.4 cm

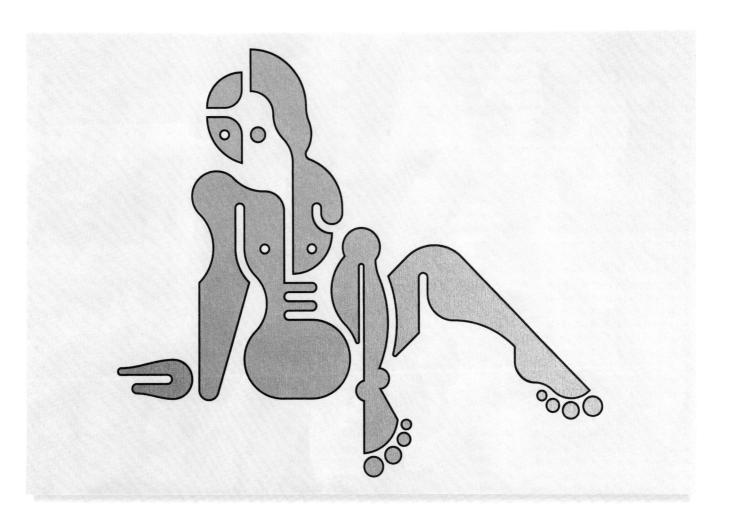

Mindscape 15, 2019
Acrylic on linen
24 x 36 inches
61 x 91.4 cm

Mindscape 16, 2019
Acrylic and metal leaf on linen
48 x 36 inches
121.9 x 91.4 cm

Mindscape 17, 2019
Acrylic and metal leaf on linen
12 x 72 inches
30.5 x 182.9 cm

Mindscape 18, 2019
Acrylic and metal leaf on linen
36 x 48 inches
91.4 x 121.9 cm

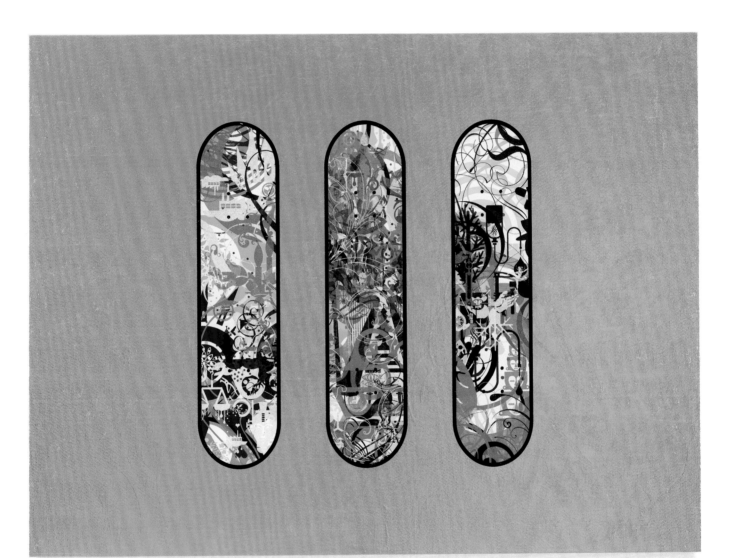

Mindscape 19, 2019
Acrylic and metal leaf on linen
36 x 48 inches
91.4 x 121.9 cm

Mindscape 20, 2019
Acrylic on linen
72 x 12 inches
182.9 x 30.5 cm

Mindscape 21, 2019
Acrylic on linen
24 x 24 inches
61 x 61 cm

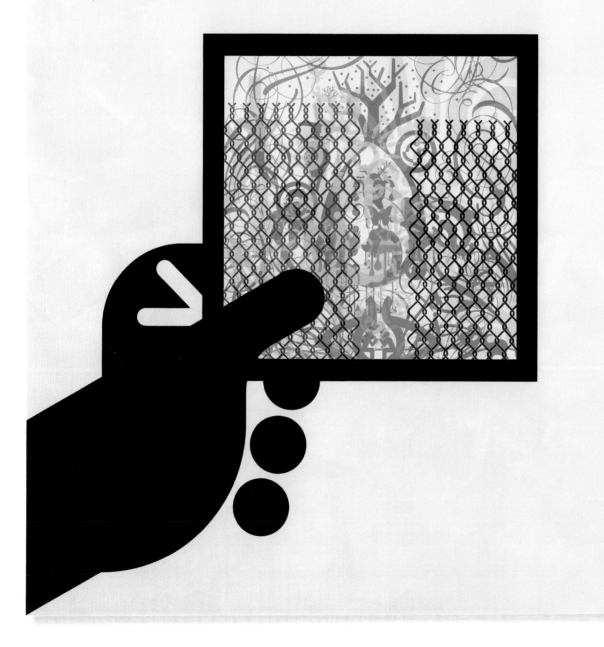

Mindscape 22, 2019
Acrylic and metal leaf on linen
24 x 24 inches
61 x 61 cm

Mindscape 23, 2019
Acrylic and metal leaf on linen
48 x 48 inches
121.9 x 121.9 cm

Mindscape 24, 2019
Acrylic and metal leaf on linen
36 x 72 inches
91.4 x 182.9 cm

Mindscape 25, 2019
Acrylic on linen
36 x 72 inches
91.4 x 182.9 cm

Mindscape 26, 2019
Acrylic and metal leaf on linen
72 x 72 inches
182.9 x 182.9 cm

Mindscape 27, 2019
Acrylic and metal leaf on linen
72 x 31 inches
182.9 x 78.7 cm

Mindscape 28, 2019
Acrylic and metal leaf on linen
72 x 36 inches
182.9 x 91.4 cm

Mindscape 29, 2019
Acrylic on linen
24 x 24 inches
61 x 61 cm

Mindscape 30, 2019
Acrylic and metal leaf on linen
24 x 24 inches
61 x 61 cm

Mindscape 31, 2019
Acrylic and metal leaf on linen
24 x 24 inches
61 x 61 cm

Mindscape 32, 2019
Acrylic and metal leaf on linen
72 x 36 inches
182.9 x 91.4 cm

Mindscape 33, 2019
Acrylic and metal leaf on linen
24 x 36 inches
61 x 91.4 cm

Mindscape 34, 2019
Acrylic and metal leaf on linen
24 x 36 inches
61 x 91.4 cm

Mindscape 35, 2019
Acrylic and metal leaf on linen
24 x 36 inches
61 x 91.4 cm

Mindscape 36, 2019
Acrylic on linen
72 x 12 inches
182.9 x 30.5 cm

Mindscape 37, 2019
Acrylic on linen
72 x 12 inches
182.9 x 30.5 cm

Mindscape 38, 2019
Acrylic and metal leaf on linen
48 x 48 inches
121.9 x 121.9 cm

Mindscape 39, 2019
Acrylic and metal leaf on linen
24 x 24 inches
61 x 61 cm

Mindscape 40, 2019
Acrylic on linen
24 x 24 inches
61 x 61 cm

Mindscape 41, 2019
Acrylic on linen
36 x 24 inches
91.4 x 61 cm

Mindscape 42, 2019
Acrylic and metal leaf on linen
36 x 24 inches
91.4 x 61 cm

Mindscape 43, 2019
Acrylic and metal leaf on linen
72 x 23 inches
182.9 x 58.4 cm

Mindscape 44, 2019
Acrylic and metal leaf on linen
72 x 40 inches
182.9 x 101.6 cm

Mindscape 45, 2019
Acrylic and metal leaf on linen
72 x 36 inches
182.9 x 91.4 cm

Mindscape 46, 2019
Acrylic and metal leaf on linen
24 x 36 inches
61 x 91.4 cm

Mindscape 47, 2019
Acrylic on linen
24 x 36 inches
61 x 91.4 cm

Mindscape 48, 2019
Acrylic and metal leaf on linen
24 x 36 inches
61 x 91.4 cm

Mindscape 49, 2019
Acrylic on linen
72 x 12 inches
182.9 x 30.5 cm

Mindscape 50, 2019
Acrylic and metal leaf on linen
72 x 72 inches
182.9 x 182.9 cm

Mindscape 51, 2019
Acrylic and metal leaf on linen
36 x 36 inches
91.4 x 91.4 cm

Mindscape 52, 2019
Acrylic and metal leaf on linen
36 x 36 inches
91.4 x 91.4 cm

Mindscape 53, 2019
Acrylic on linen
72 x 36 inches
182.9 x 91.4 cm

Mindscape 54, 2019
Acrylic and metal leaf on linen
24 x 24 inches
61 x 61 cm

Mindscape 55, 2019
Acrylic and metal leaf on linen
24 x 24 inches
61 x 61 cm

Mindscape 56, 2019
Acrylic and metal leaf on linen
24 x 24 inches
61 x 61 cm

Mindscape 57, 2019
Acrylic and metal leaf on linen
36 x 36 inches
91.4 x 91.4 cm

Mindscape 58, 2019
Acrylic and metal leaf on linen
36 x 36 inches
91.4 x 91.4 cm

Mindscape 59, 2019
Acrylic on linen
12 x 72 inches
30.5 x 182.9 cm

Mindscape 60, 2019
Acrylic on linen
36 x 36 inches
91.4 x 91.4 cm

Mindscape 61, 2019
Acrylic and metal leaf on linen
36 x 36 inches
91.4 x 91.4 cm

Mindscape 62, 2019
Acrylic on linen
72 x 12 inches
182.9 x 30.5 cm

Mindscape 63, 2019
Acrylic and metal leaf on linen
72 x 37 inches
182.9 x 94 cm

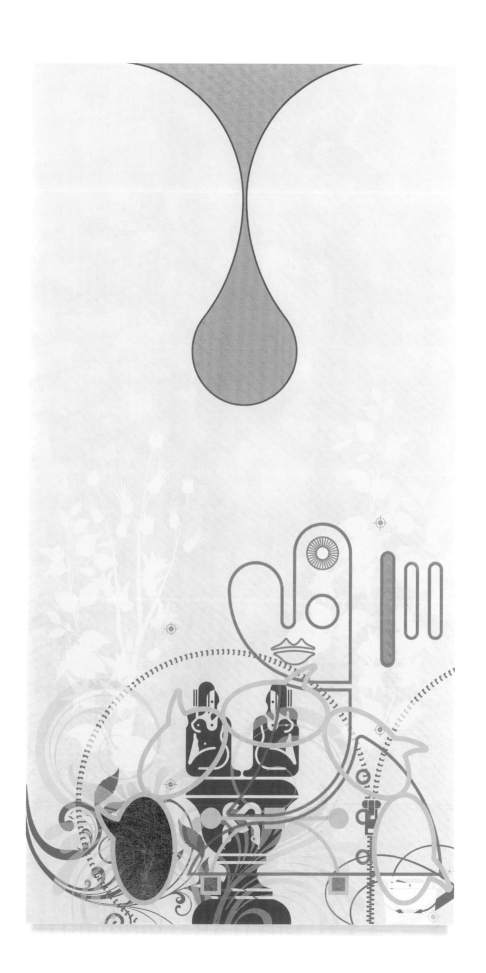

Mindscape 64, 2019
Acrylic and metal leaf on linen
72 x 32 inches
182.9 x 81.3 cm

Mindscape 65, 2019
Acrylic on linen
72 x 12 inches
182.9 x 30.5 cm

Mindscape 66, 2019
Acrylic and metal leaf on linen
36 x 60 inches
91.4 x 152.4 cm

Mindscape 67, 2019
Acrylic on linen
36 x 60 inches
91.4 x 152.4 cm

Mindscape 68, 2019
Acrylic on linen
72 x 12 inches
182.9 x 30.5 cm

Mindscape 69, 2019
Acrylic on linen
24 x 36 inches
61 x 91.4 cm

Mindscape 70, 2019
Acrylic and metal leaf on linen
24 x 36 inches
61 x 91.4 cm

Mindscape 71, 2019
Acrylic on linen
24 x 36 inches
61 x 91.4 cm

Mindscape 72, 2019
Acrylic and metal leaf on linen
72 x 72 inches
182.9 x 182.9 cm

Mindscape 1, 2019
Acrylic on linen
24 x 36 inches
61 x 91.4 cm

Mindscape 2, 2019
Acrylic and metal leaf on linen
48 x 36 inches
121.9 x 91.4 cm

Mindscape 3, 2019
Acrylic and metal leaf on linen
72 x 12 inches
182.9 x 30.5 cm

Example Combination

Mindscape 4, 2019
Acrylic and metal leaf on linen
36 x 36 inches
91.4 x 91.4 cm

Mindscape 5, 2019
Acrylic and metal leaf on linen
36 x 36 inches
91.4 x 91.4 cm

Example Combination

Mindscape 7, 2019
Acrylic and metal leaf on linen
72 x 24 inches
182.9 x 61 cm

Mindscape 8, 2019
Acrylic and metal leaf on linen
72 x 36 inches
182.9 x 91.4 cm

Example Combination

Mindscape 36, 2019
Acrylic on linen
72 x 12 inches
182.9 x 30.5 cm

Mindscape 37, 2019
Acrylic on linen
72 x 12 inches
182.9 x 30.5 cm

Example Combination

180

Mindscape 44, 2019
Acrylic and metal leaf on linen
72 x 40 inches
182.9 x 101.6 cm

Mindscape 45, 2019
Acrylic and metal leaf on linen
72 x 36 inches
182.9 x 91.4 cm

Example Combination

Mindscape 46, 2019
Acrylic and metal leaf on linen
24 x 36 inches
61 x 91.4 cm

Mindscape 47, 2019
Acrylic on linen
24 x 36 inches
61 x 91.4 cm

Mindscape 48, 2019
Acrylic and metal leaf on linen
24 x 36 inches
61 x 91.4 cm

Example Combination

Mindscape 51, 2019
Acrylic and metal leaf on linen
36 x 36 inches
91.4 x 91.4 cm

Mindscape 52, 2019
Acrylic and metal leaf on linen
36 x 36 inches
91.4 x 91.4 cm

Example Combination

Mindscape 57, 2019
Acrylic and metal leaf on linen
36 x 36 inches
91.4 x 91.4 cm

Mindscape 58, 2019
Acrylic and metal leaf on linen
36 x 36 inches
91.4 x 91.4 cm

Mindscape 59, 2019
Acrylic on linen
12 x 72 inches
30.5 x 182.9 cm

Example Combination

Mindscape 60, 2019
Acrylic on linen
36 x 36 inches
91.4 x 91.4 cm

Mindscape 61, 2019
Acrylic and metal leaf on linen
36 x 36 inches
91.4 x 91.4 cm

Example Combination

Mindscape 64, 2019
Acrylic and metal leaf on linen
72 x 32 inches
182.9 x 81.3 cm

Mindscape 65, 2019
Acrylic on linen
72 x 12 inches
182.9 x 30.5 cm

Example Combination

Mindscape 69, 2019
Acrylic on linen
24 x 36 inches
61 x 91.4 cm

Mindscape 70, 2019
Acrylic and metal leaf on linen
24 x 36 inches
61 x 91.4 cm

Mindscape 71, 2019
Acrylic on linen
24 x 36 inches
61 x 91.4 cm

THE WARHOL CONNECTION

Eric Shiner Interviews Ryan McGinness
New York City, Fall 2019

ERIC SHINER: We've known each other for quite some time. Let's start there. If you remember, we first met in Tokyo, which must have been sometime around 2000.

RYAN McGINNESS: Maybe even a little later. Maybe 2001. I was doing an exhibition there.

ES: At Parco Museum, if I remember correctly. That makes sense, because that is when I was in Japan on the ground, and had moved there in 1998 to go to graduate school in Osaka, but I still made my forays to Tokyo. And when I heard that you were there, I literally showed up at the gallery and knocked on the door. I don't know if there was anyone else there other than you installing. I remember the skateboards and toy soldier pieces.

Top Left: *Supreme Color Formula Guide*, 2000, silkscreen on skateboards, 32 x 8 inches (81.3 x 20.3 cm) ea., published by Supreme, New York
Top Right: *Saving Ryan's Privates (Target)*, 2000, plastic toy soldiers on wood panel, 36 x 36 x 4 inches (91.4 x 91.4 x 10.2 cm)
Bottom: *Evolution Is the Theory of Everything*, 2001, installation view, Parco Museum, Tokyo, Japan

RM: I was making paintings on skateboards using oil enamel and vinyl. And color-field paintings with thousands of toy soldiers.

ES: The reason that I went was because I knew that we had something in common and that something was Pittsburgh and The Andy Warhol Museum, specifically. It was very interesting for me to find out that we literally missed each other by a matter of probably days, because you were the official first intern of The Andy Warhol Museum.

RM: I interned there in the fall of 1993 and spring of 1994. I helped them move into the building renovated by Richard Gluckman on the Northside of Pittsburgh. I designed some of the first print materials for the museum, because I was studying graphic design at Carnegie Mellon University. I remember Tom Armstrong. I think he was the first director there.

ES: Mark Francis was the founding director, but he quickly decided to be the Chief Curator, and that is when they brought in Tom Armstrong from the Whitney Museum.

RM: I remember Tom was so nice to everyone who worked there, including us interns. I even brought my slide sheet in to have him look at my paintings. I was making paintings of public domain "clip art" drawings. I don't remember him dismissing the work, but I also don't remember him offering me a show. My internship ended on the day that the museum opened, which was the weekend of my graduation. That weekend in May 1994, I went to the grand opening of The Andy Warhol Museum, graduated from Carnegie Mellon University, and moved to Manhattan.

Nurse Alien, 1994, mixed pigments on wood, 31 x 22 inches (78.7 x 55.9 cm)

Hostage Bunny, 1994, mixed pigments on canvas, 36 x 36 inches (91.4 x 91.4 cm)

Warhol Flower Icon (WFI.48.7), 2018, acrylic on linen, 48 x 48 inches (121.9 x 121.9 cm)

ES: Which is so absolutely incredible, not dissimilar from Andy graduating from Carnegie Tech back in the day and leaving for New York in a matter of a few weeks.

RM: Our careers paralleled in that he did commercial design work upon arriving in New York as well. That is how I stayed alive. I designed logos, album covers, and posters.

ES: Absolutely, as did he, most decidedly. It is very interesting, because we were both at the opening of the Andy Warhol Museum that night. So we were there at the same time, and yet we didn't know each other. And while you were volunteering in the offices of The Andy Warhol Museum at the Carnegie, I was volunteering in the Japanese print department at the Carnegie.

RM: Your trajectory there is really interesting because you went from intern to director. How did that happen?

ES: I studied 16th century Japanese screen painting and castle architecture as an undergraduate, and lived in Japan for a year and was gone for another semester at sea. But I was so intrigued by things Japanese and thinking about aesthetics and military force and power and all of the things that I ended up writing about. Luckily for me, because of that relationship with the Carnegie, I was asked if I would be an intern at the Warhol museum. What a wonderful year it was.

RM: You were a fan of Warhol.

ES: I was a fan of Warhol.

RM: You were just being modest when you said, "I don't know anything about Warhol..."

ES: Well, I knew soup cans and Marilyn Monroe and a few other things. But I also knew that he was from Pittsburgh like me and I also knew that he was gay. I had just come out of the closet, in my senior year of college. Luckily I was able to meld my love of Japan and Warhol and start looking at post-war Japanese art, which is ultimately what I did. Which is what took me to Japan to go to graduate school, studying post-war Japanese art, but through the lens of Warhol so I wrote my thesis on Morimura Yasumasa looking at gender, looking at pop, looking at fame. And those were the things that I talked about, not only with his work and his contemporaries, but I also then traced it back, things like gender transformation and mythology, through centuries of Japanese art. So, I was able to triangulate and bring all of this together.

RM: Now I understand why you were interested in my *Warhol Flower Icons* and the assertions I want to make in the forthcoming book on the *Flowers*—about the stamen in particular and how they are super subversive.

ES: And how you have certainly boiled that down to a code, almost, in your work, is incredibly interesting. That is what fueled my passion for so long. Thinking about other artworks in the world and Warhol's place within them. Because Warhol certainly became one of the most famous artists the world has ever known and one of the most famous people the world has ever known. And nearly every artist has to reckon with Warhol, in one way, shape, or form. Love him or hate him, I have always been very impressed that you have the bravado to dive right in, because very few artists are able and willing to do that.

RM: Well, only after a long time. For 20 years, Warhol has often been evoked when addressing my work. And, usually for very superficial reasons, primarily because of silkscreening. I have had anxiety and mixed feelings about living in the shadow of Warhol. I mean, we all live in his shadow. I never really wanted to be in the shadow of anyone. My point is, only recently have I felt compelled to address Warhol in my work, head-on. It is time. I can accept it. So then, the question is, why the flowers? I think they are fascinating, misunderstood, underappreciated, and often dismissed as being purely decorative. They were made very sarcastically. What happens to an artwork when its original intention dissolves away over the years?

ES: Warhol's sense of humor was huge. It so often goes away. It was sharp. It was dirty. It was really pointed.

RM: Yes, and so subversive. Many of those intentions dissolve. And so, what is the value of trying to make people aware of the original intentions of artworks?

ES: It's the very thing that art history does. But also, on that front, you re-analyzing Warhol is not dissimilar from Warhol re-analyzing Duchamp, which he was doing constantly. He's thinking about appropriation, he's thinking about the ready-made, he's thinking about things from mainstream society through the lens of Duchamp, and also thinking about things like the shadow and humor. These are constants in Warhol, and it's all coming from Duchamp. But, he too had a certain sense of disbelief meets not a huge amount of confidence in taking on Duchamp, who's the great master of Modernism as we know it, and we open the door to say that literally anything could be considered a work of art. Warhol seemingly threw that door open, blasted it off the hinges, and rolled with it even further. But, it's all coming from a very Duchampian position. Where are you on Duchamp?

Untitled (Bicycle Wheel, After Marcel Duchamp), 2019, digital vector file

RM: Duchamp is another shadow-casting artist. No artist can escape him. In fact, last week, I just finished another drawing of one of his works, *Bicycle Wheel*, which is on view at the newly re-opened MoMA now. You know, I'm always making new drawings to add to my vocabulary. That one will get thrown into the mix for these new *Mindscape* paintings.

ES: In so many ways, you're the logical grandchild of Duchamp by making symbols—perfectly, immediately understood symbols—and turning them into your own language.

RM: Yes, using the forms of international standard icons as a ready-made language.

ES: Exactly.

RM: I am always careful to point out that my ingredients are homegrown and original. Appropriation is a cul-de-sac, you know, a dead-end. I'd rather be the artist who is appropriated than the one appropriating. However, the irony is that I make these drawings that look as if they've been appropriated.

ES: They're completely original and your own. Warhol was very much the same way in that he did, of course, appropriate images, but he skewed them so much making them his own, that he really takes them out of the world of reality and propels them into a totally different place. That's certainly always been very intriguing to me. I think it's also very much the reason why so many people are able to relate to Warhol, in that, like your work, there are distinct and direct ties to the world that we live in, and the time that we are living, that makes things that much more accessible, but also allows one to escape from the reality of the world.

RM: I suppose that is always the balance in the artist's role: World creation within the context of a world that already exists. How do we create new original worlds that are unique unto the creator? If the work is not the product of a specific individual spirit, then to what degree do we value it as art? There is a spectrum to which I am alluding that demonstrates the difference between artist and art director. This is a debate Warhol celebrated. Of course, he was much more of a process artist than many believe.

ES: It is a huge mythology that he wasn't involved in his work, and it's one that he put forward himself to try to make people think that he was an actual machine or that he had other people making his art.

RM: That's one of the biggest misconceptions about Warhol. And this goes back to what we were saying about how intentions dissolve. Andy's assertion that he wanted to be a machine and that anyone could make his work was the critique. I'm so disappointed in artists who take a factory-like approach to making their work and think they're being Warholian. His interest in manipulating materials and process came from his graphic arts background. He may not have been the best silk-screener in the world, and I often find myself getting hung up on his misuse of halftones against the incorrect screen mesh, but those are my own obsessions. No one can deny the fact that he was involved in the process. Even the decision to not make decisions is a decision. It comes down to being accountable and responsible for the work. Being an artist means assuming undiluted accountability and responsibility for the work.

ES: We all know that he was there constantly, but he also certainly was not a perfectionist by any stretch of the imagination, and he allowed for and celebrated the chance that the sloppiness of the screen and pulling the squeegee down would enact onto the canvas. So for him, sometimes the messier the better.

RM: That's one of the reasons why the work needs to be seen in person, although it is designed for reproduction. There are subtleties that are being declared. Additionally,

Ryan McGinness in Studio, Photo by Jennifer Livingston for Wall Street Journal

his use of fluorescents and materials like diamond dust force a real-world experience. As does scale.

ES: Fully agreed. It's a constant.

RM: Let's go back to your internship at the Warhol Museum. After that, you left?

ES: I left the museum, and I worked at a non-profit in Pittsburgh—the Japan-America Society of Pennsylvania. I did that for a year, and then I went to work at the University of Pittsburgh for two years running a thing called the Japanese Science and Technology Management Program. I left in spring of 1998 to move to Osaka, where I started my master's degree in postwar Japanese art history, and that brings me through 2001. That's when I became the assistant curator for the Yokohama Triennale. After that, I had a job offer from a museum in Tokyo, and I also was able to have the great benefit of being accepted into Yale for the PhD program to start later that year. So I needed to decide do I stay in Japan and build my curatorial practice and career here? Or, do I go back to the states and go down the academic path? I decided to come back to the states. I had known Xu Bing, the Chinese artist, since the nineties from Pittsburgh and knew Cai Guo-Qiang in Japan, and met

Ai Wei Wei around that time. So I very quickly realized that I was one of the few people in America that actually knew a lot about Asian contemporary art. So, as it was exploding here in the city, I made the very tough decision to leave school. I got a master's degree out of the deal and moved to New York at the end of that summer, and hit the ground running, and had four incredible years of curating, writing, editing.

RM: So you were doing all that on a freelance basis?

ES: I was doing that freelance, I had a day job at a non-profit called the Alliance for the Arts, it was a cultural promotion agency for the arts in the city and New York state. It was a fantastic base of operations. Luckily, as things were building up, two years later, I went fully independent and did everything on my own for two years. But it was a wonderful, wonderful ride. It allowed me to travel to Asia extensively, and I was the Managing Editor of Art Asia Pacific magazine, I was writing for auction houses, for galleries, curating exhibitions and really riding the wave of the newfound love for Asian contemporary art, which was a very thrilling time. Luckily, the summer before 2008, I received a call from The Andy Warhol Museum asking how I'd feel about going home to be the Chief Curator. Needless to say, I said "Yes" immediately. It would be a dream come true. Where were you in 2008?

RM: I was still in New York. I was doing solo shows at the Cincinnati Art Museum, MoMA PS1, a gallery show in Milan, and preparing for my last solo show at Deitch Projects in New York.

ES: Because when you left Pittsburgh, you moved to New York. And you haven't lived anywhere else?

RM: Exactly. I've been in Manhattan for 25 years.

ES: Just for the record, why don't you talk a little bit about where you are from and how you got to where you are, and how you made your way to Pittsburgh for college.

RM: Well, it's very simple and linear. I grew up in Virginia Beach—kindergarten through twelfth grade. I went to a Gifted and Talented school one day a week for art. So, from a very early age, art was a serious academic discipline. For me, art was never an extra-curricular easy-A,

Flocci Non Facio, 2004, installation view, *Beautiful Losers* exhibition, Contemporary Arts Center Cincinnati

Have You Seen Him?, 2008, installation view, MoMA PS1, New York, Photo by Tom Powel Imaging

Ryan McGinness Works, 2009, installation view, Deitch Projects, New York, Photo by Tom Powel Imaging

the way it is often positioned in public school. It was a difficult program. In elementary school, we were given college-level art history exams. I remember not being allowed to go outside for recess until I finished a still life. I craved that kind of seriousness.

ES: Did the Chrysler Museum play any role along the line?

Kindergarten Report Card, 1978, John B. Dey Elementary School, Virginia Beach, VA

Communication through Art, cover page for elementary school essay, 1984

Spread from junior high school yearbook showing McGinness as a member of both the Computer Club and Art Club, 1985, Great Neck Junior High School, Virginia Beach, VA

Art History is Not Linear, 2014, installation view, Virginia Museum of Fine Arts, Richmond, VA. Photo by David Stover. Courtesy Virginia Museum of Fine Arts

RM: Sure, of course. We would go on field trips to the Chrysler Museum in nearby Norfolk and to the Virginia Museum of Fine Arts in Richmond. But, in Virginia Beach, there were no museums. The Virginia Museum of Contemporary Art opened the year I left.

ES: There were no programs for promising youth like Andy had at the Carnegie Museum?

RM: No, but I always had a sense of there being some other kind of more formal art world out there. I got a sense of that from, you know, not only these museum field trips but also Warhol's *Interview* magazine. The Old Donation Center for the Gifted and Talented had a subscription to *Interview* magazine, so I would get to go through a new issue every month. That was like a glimpse into another world.

ES: Same here. I think for so many of us, the thought about a world beyond our own immediate environment, magazines in general, were certainly a great conduit to learning about the world beyond. But I think *Interview* magazine for so many of us was the epitome of New York cool. Those of us that saw that cool really used that as a vehicle to one day end up here.

RM: Agreed. So, I continued to study art seriously through high school, but I also did very well academically. Unlike most artists who often pride themselves on being an outsider or loser, I was my class president, I was captain of the debate team, I was the National Honor Society president, took AP classes. I did all of that stuff.

ES: Same, same. I was treasurer, not president, but all of the others, yes.

High school band flyer, photocopier toner on paper, c. 1988

Design foundation studies, plaka paint with ruling pen on illustration boards, Carnegie Mellon University, 1991

RM: So you get it! Isn't it silly how the cliché of the outcast artist is often embraced? So, I was conflicted between an academic pursuit and an art pursuit, until I discovered this thing called "graphic design." It was a discipline that I could grab onto and something concrete I could learn. It had rules, systems, experimentation with control groups, typography, communication, goals, and accountability. I realized that design was at the core of a lot of my pursuits, like with student election campaign flyers and posters, presentation materials. I would design report covers before writing my reports. And I was in a band, but had no musical talent. I liked making the cassette covers, flyers, t-shirts, and other band propaganda. I also had an after-school job at one of the military bases in Virginia Beach, where I was an artist-illustrator. I made flyers, posters, and newsletters.

ES: Wow, like Phillip Pearlstein! In the military, that's what saved his life because he literally took some of his drawings from Carnegie Mellon, from his first year because he was drafted and he showed his supervisor these drawings and said "this is what I want to do" and they saw talent and they found him a role, and they didn't put him into the field.

RM: Well, my stint in the military, as a civilian, may have only saved me from an existential crisis of what to be. That job gave me access to photocopiers and Kroy lettering machines, and I started to learn principles of layout using wax machines doing paste-ups. That job helped foster my passion, and I went off to the design program at Carnegie Mellon University. I also studied art, of course, but all my studio classes were in design. I was all-in during that time. I started taking on freelance jobs while a sophomore, and I spent my summers in

Pittsburgh working at a design firm and a public-relations firm. I could not get enough of school and work. I remember just always wanting more, and that hunger carried over to New York. I made paintings and showed anywhere and everywhere.

ES: You did exactly what I what I tell artists to constantly do, and curators, would-be-artists and would-be-curators. If there is a wall, fill it. Don't be afraid to go out there, make the connection, and get your work on the wall because you never know when you're going to be discovered. Who discovered you as an artist?

RM: Oh, I don't even know if I like that idea of discovery, especially as it applies to humans.

ES: Well, who was the first person in the art world who took notice?

RM: My peers. That's the best answer. To have the recognition of your peers is the best kind of recognition. I exhibited at Alife on the Lower East Side, Colette in Paris, Houston Gallery in Seattle, and eventually at more formal galleries like Deitch Projects.

ES: So when did Jeffrey first find you?

RM: I first showed there in 2002. I had a few books that were circulating by that time.

ES: You really love making books. You've made so many wonderful books.

RM: I can't help it. They just happen. Making a book is the same as making a painting. I've made books since

Part of Everything, 2000, enamel on 360 canvas boards,
96 x 480 inches (91.4 x 1219.2 cm), installation view, Alife, New York

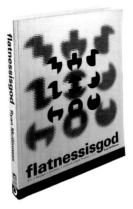

Flatnessisgod, 1999, 11 x 8½ inches (27.9 x 21.6 cm), 1C, 256pp., softcover,
first edition published by Soft Skull Press and Razorfish, ISBN: 1-887128-34-4

grade school. One of my thesis projects at CMU was called "What is a Book?" and I would do silly things, as a precocious art student, like turn a room into a book by making the door the cover. The environment of the room was the content and the experience of the room was the "reading" of the book. Anyway, yes, I love making books. My first book, *Flatnessisgod* came out in 1999. It did well in Japan, and that's how I met Takashi Murakami. He interviewed me on his radio show and bought some of my paintings. His *Superflat* book came out the next year.

ES: So, with this show, what is your goal, and what do you want to say to the world?

RM: I haven't really done anything in New York for a while. You know my whole idea behind that, and just being super careful about what I do in my hometown, because it matters most to me. Meanwhile, I've been happy to do anything and everything outside New York, and that's what I've been doing. So, what I hope to do with the show is put my best foot forward. I'm pushing some new materials and new images within what I call the *Mindscapes* body of work. These are the more surreal and psychedelic-influenced works as opposed to the more figurative works or *Black Holes*, for example. The "statements" are contained within the individual iconic drawings, which I consider the units of meaning. These get crushed together within the picture planes to reflect how our minds work—random access memories. RAM is also how computer memories work. Meanings are constructed by the viewer or user. Now, formally,

my goal is to make one strong large statement painting comprised of smaller discrete paintings that work on their own. The exhibition, will therefore, be one large painting that wraps around the entire perimeter of the gallery, but it also breaks down to separate paintings of different sizes. There are 72 paintings total. I was born in 1972. And, this structural strategy satisfies the final goal, which is to make market-friendly works. After all, the exhibition is in an art store. It's a sophisticated art store, but still, we're all bearing the burden of the expenses involved in producing this exhibition. And, I have a lot of mouths to feed, as Andy said.

ES: Absolutely. I think it's very important on that note to say, and to remind artists, that to make money from one's work is the goal—to support yourself and to thrive. Because artists have for far too long played into the romantic notion of the starving artist, which isn't really fun for anybody, and Warhol certainly blew that out of the water and did incredibly well in his lifetime.

RM: And that's why he was criticized so much.

ES: It was the criticism that he was a sell-out. I always viewed it more of him buying in and getting other people to buy in, which is one of the great twists, one of the great schemes that an artist can pull on society, by getting people to pay for your idea and your concept.

RM: It has only been within the past five years or so that I've come to terms with this revelation: Only the market will protect the work. Museums can't protect work anymore. Only the market can protect what we value in culture. The problem, of course, is that the market follows what is popular, not what is good or critically acclaimed. This is how civilizations begin to crumble.

ES: It's the way it is, it's the way it has always been, that the artists that we continue to talk about, whether in life or in death, met market success to the degree that the objects that they made became as valuable to society as real estate, as stock, as gold. That these things were so valued because of their beauty, their making, their content. That those with power and those with wealth decided centuries ago that these things mattered, and people sadly forget this. That, I think is the ultimate victory of artists, that one's vision, one's voice, one's work, now one's labor, is as critical to the concept of value in society as any of the great areas of wealth accumulation—gold, real estate, stocks—art even surpasses those, and I think that it's the greatest of ironies that artists and their radicality and their craziness and their eccentricities and their quest to break rules ultimately go on to become the most valued names and objects in the world.

RM: It seems ironic, but instead of being trapped by money, art transcends money. Whatever price is paid for an artwork, it will always be a good deal. It doesn't matter. You can never pay too much for art because it is an attempt to capture something with a system that simply does not apply. Market exchange is a coarse net, and art is too fine for it.

ES: Absolutely. If it is valued and if it is believed in. It's a belief system.

RM: When money doesn't apply, all you're left with is faith. Money will never catch up to faith, but it tries. History tells us that.

ES: Agreed. Especially when it's something that you love and that you value and that society agrees with through all the many mechanisms including museums, including galleries, including magazines, including many of the things we've talked about today that support and propel an artist's voice and an artist's work. But, at the end of the day, it's really just about these base concepts of belief and value.

RM: I've always thought that art should be priced as a percentage of one's income. It makes value not about a specific dollar amount, but about a relative cost, or pain, we are each willing to endure in exchange for a work of art. Are you willing to pay 10% of your income? 50%? Do I hear 90%? I bet you'd be surprised by how many of the current top art collectors in the world would not be willing to collect based on that model. And, many poor people would become contenders at the auctions. Collectors would then be seen as heroes for their sacrifice for protecting art. That is one way to democratize art purchasing.

ES: As with most things in life, the great things surface to the top and will be remembered. And I think that you will be that.

RM: Thanks. I think "great things" are those which we find meaningful. I've become obsessed with not only meaning, but the meaning of meaning and how meaning is attributed. Why have we evolved to seek meaning? These curiosities are being poured into the new work. Meaning requires participation. Participation comes from attraction. I need to make attractive work that then delivers upon visitation.

ES: Absolutely, I hope that with this show you set a wonderful trap that viewers will only have the option to fall into.

RM: Yes, I like that word "trap," because I am trying to use beauty as a Trojan Horse.

ES: Exactly.

RM: And so, I'm often thrown when people say, "Oh your work is so beautiful." I feel like, "Thank goodness you didn't go in!" because there are the horrors of bad trips and dreams and suicide in there. And some nice things. And something things. And nothing things.

ES: But as it is true that viewers will all come to a work, and your work especially, with their own histories, their own traumas, their own joys. And I think that is another reason that like Andy you were able to connect with such a large audience because you do set this all out, there are so many connection points that one can make. And each person will have a different experience in front of each work, and some will fall into the trap of beauty and remain there, whereas others will see the complexities and the depth and the darkness that revise that, and have a completely bordering on, perhaps bordering spiritual connection to the work and this is the beauty of the art world and that there are no correct ways to address a work or to connect to a work.

RM: I think what you're getting at is so important. The best thing about art is that there are no rules. As soon as people start making up rules, then you must break them to remind people that there are no rules. The best art reminds people that there are no rules about art.

ES: Exactly, and luckily for all of us, the great artists are the ones that broke the rules harder than anyone, and those are the voices that we celebrate. The true radicals of a given age.

RM: I so appreciate when someone brings into question my aesthetic, my visual language, and tries to dismiss it as out of bounds for art. That means I am doing something right. Mine is an aesthetic that is rooted in another field—in the service industry of graphic design. When I employ it for my own means of expression, and it is met with resistance, well, that's perfect.

Anyway, let's bring this conversation back to how we've known each other over the years. We were in 2008 when you were the curator at The Andy Warhol Museum. You brought me into a group show there.

ES: It was *Factory Direct: Pittsburgh*, so that must have been just a few years after that, in 2012. *Factory Direct* was about thinking how an artist can collaborate with either a factory or a scientist, or a researcher, and to throw the artist into this new world and encourage artists to collaborate with someone outside of their own immediate world, to make a new work of art, and boy, were the results phenomenal across the board, and certainly challenging for both the artist and the collaborators on the other side trying to find a common language.

Women (Forms + Surfaces 1), 2012, etched mirror-polished stainless steel, 30 ¼ x 22 inches (76.8 x 55.9 cm)

RM: That show was such a treat to be a part of and thank you again for inviting me.

ES: Thank you for doing it.

RM: Especially because it was a rare instance where, as far as the logistics went, you took care of everything. You made it so easy for that collaboration to happen. It doesn't always go that way.

ES: No, it definitely doesn't. And you also had wonderful collaborators in the company, Forms and Surfaces. The very name was so perfect for you and for your practice. It was great that everyone bonded, and it allowed you to think about making artwork in new materials and through new technologies that they were trying to perfect.

RM: Yes. So, that's when we connected more recently, 2012, and since then as your career has progressed beyond the museum. Beyond Warhol.

ES: Absolutely. To be sure. As we will continue to be.

Eric Shiner is the inaugural Executive Director of *Pioneer Works* in Red Hook, Brooklyn. He was most recently Artistic Director of *White Cube*, New York and prior to this was a Senior Vice President of Contemporary Art at *Sotheby's*. From 2010 to 2016, Shiner was the director of *The Andy Warhol Museum* in Pittsburgh and was the Milton Fine Curator of Art at *The Warhol* from 2008 to 2010. A leading scholar on Andy Warhol and Asian contemporary art, Shiner lived and worked in Japan for a total of six years and was assistant curator on the inaugural *Yokohama Triennale* in 2001.

RYAN McGINNESS

Born in Virginia Beach, VA in 1972
Lives and works in New York, NY

EDUCATION

1994
BFA, Carnegie Mellon University, Pittsburgh, PA

1990–1994
Curatorial Assistant, Andy Warhol Museum,
    Pittsburgh, PA

SELECT SOLO EXHIBITIONS

2020
"Mindscapes," Miles McEnery Gallery, New York, NY

2019
"Warhol Flower Icons," Baldwin Gallery, Aspen, CO
"Mother & Child," Harper's Books, East Hampton, NY

2018
"Warhol Flower Icons," Aisho Nanzuka,
    Hong Kong, China
"Warhol Flower Icons," EchoOne Nanzuka,
    Bangkok, Thailand

2017
"Studio Views," Cranbrook Art Museum,
    Bloomfield Hills, MI
"Ocular Evidence," Quint Gallery, San Diego, CA

2016
"#metadata," Kohn Gallery, Los Angeles, CA

2015
"Ryan McGinness: Studio Visit," Virginia Museum
    of Contemporary Art, Virginia Beach, VA

2014
"Community Identity Stability," Quint Gallery,
    La Jolla, CA
"Figure Drawings," Pace Prints, New York, NY

"Everything Is Everywhere," Galerie Ron Mandos,
    Amsterdam, The Netherlands
"Art History Is Not Linear (Boijmans)," Vous Etes Ici,
    Amsterdam, The Netherlands
"Ryan McGinness: Studio Visit," Virginia Museum of
    Fine Arts, Richmond, VA

2013
"Women & Mindscapes," Galerie Forsblom,
    Helsinki, Finland

2012
"Women: New (Re)Presentations," Quint Gallery,
    La Jolla, CA
"Women: Sun-Stained Symbols," Glenn Horowitz
    Bookseller, East Hampton, NY
"Units of Meaning," Baldwin Gallery, Aspen, CO
"Women: Sketches & Solutions," Gering & López Gallery,
    New York, NY
"Geometric Primitives," Pace Primitive, New York, NY

2011
"Trophies," Prism Gallery, Los Angeles, CA
"Works on Paper," Country Club, Los Angeles, CA
"Recent Paintings," Kohn Gallery, Los Angeles, CA
"Color Oblicuo," Espai Cultural Caja Madrid,
    Madrid, Spain
"Black Holes," Phillips de Pury & Company, New York, NY

2010
"New Tondos," Galerie Forsblom, Helsinki, Finland
"Studio Franchise," La Casa Encendida Museum,
    Madrid, Spain

2009
"Ryan McGinness Works," Deitch Projects, New York, NY
"Mindscapes & Black Holes," Baldwin Gallery,
    Aspen, CO

2008

"Ryan McGinness: Aesthetic Comfort," Cincinnati
    Art Museum, Cincinnati, OH
"A Shadow Feeling of Loss," Paolo Curti/Annamaria
    Gambuzzi and Co., Milan, Italy
"Have You Seen Him?," MoMA PS1, New York, NY

2007

"Varied Editions," Pace Prints, New York, NY
"A Rich Fantasy Life," Quint Gallery, La Jolla, CA

2006

"Never Odd Or Even," Galería Moriarty, Madrid, Spain
"Never Odd Or Even," Vous Etes Ici, Amsterdan,
    The Netherlands
"Never Odd Or Even," Paolo Curti/Annamaria
    Gambuzzi and Co., Milan, Italy
"Gas, Grass, or Ass (Nobody Rides for Free)," Glenn
    Horowitz Bookseller, East Hampton, NY
"Mildly Subversive," Montserrat College of Art Gallery,
    Beverly, MA

2005

"Installationview," Deitch Projects, New York, NY
"The Burden of Keeping it Real," André Simoens
    Gallery, Knokke-Zoute, Belgium
"Pain-Free Kittens," Quint Gallery, La Jolla, CA

2004

"Multiverse," Galerie du jour agnès b., Paris, France
"Living Signs," Galería Moriarty, Madrid, Spain

2003

"Worlds within Worlds," Deitch Projects, New York, NY
"Sponsorship," Black Market Gallery, Los Angeles, CA

2002

"This Dream Is So Life-Like," Gas Gallery, Tokyo, Japan
"Products Are The New Art," Printed Matter,
    New York, NY
"Dream Garden" (with Julia Chiang), Deitch Projects,
    New York, NY

2001

"Evolution Is the Theory of Everything," Parco Gallery,
    Tokyo, Japan

"Sign Age," Galerie de Miguel, Munich, Germany
"Pieceofmind," Colette, Paris, France

2000

"Shtick," Houston Gallery, Seattle, WA
"Luxurygood," Alife, New York, NY

SELECT GROUP EXHIBITIONS

2018

"Grafik" (curated by Ryan McGinness), Harper's Books,
    East Hampton, NY
"Heads Roll" (curated by Paul Morrison), Graves
    Gallery, Sheffield, United Kingdom
"Tick Tock: Time in Contemporary Art," Lehman
    College Art Gallery, New York, NY

2017

"Drawing: The Beginning of Everything," Albright-Knox
    Art Gallery, Buffalo, NY

2016

'Library Street Collective Presents,' Library Street
    Collective, Detroit, MI

2015

"A Perspective on Agnès B.'s Collection," Lille
    Métropole Musée d'Art Moderne, Lille, France
"Beauty Reigns: A Baroque Sensibility in Recent
    Paintings," Akron Art Museum, Akron, OH

2014

"Beauty Reigns: A Baroque Sensibility in Recent
    Painting," McNay Art Museum, San Antonio, TX

2012

"Factory Direct," The Andy Warhol Museum, Pittsburgh,
    PA
"Modern and Contemporary Art from Private
    Collections," Montclair Art Museum, Montclair, NJ

2011

"Masters of Reality," Gering & López Gallery,
    New York, NY

"Nose Job" (curated by Carlo McCormick), Eric Firestone Gallery, East Hampton, NY

"Litos Grafera," Art Centre Silkeborg Bad, Silkeborg, Denmark

"Litos Grafera," Museum of Stavanger, Stavanger, Norway

2010
"Contemporary Magic" (curated by Stacy Engman), National Arts Club, New York, NY

2008
"Royal Academy Illustrated 2008: A Selection from the 240th Summer Exhibition," Royal Academy of Arts, London, United Kingdom

2007
"Monumental Drawing," Blue Star Contemporary Art Center, San Antonio, TX

2006
"Graphic Content," Contemporary Art Center, Cincinnati, OH

"Art on Paper 2006," Weatherspoon Art Museum, Greensboro, NC

"The World Is Round," Public Art Fund, MetroTech, Brooklyn, NY

"USA Today: New American Art from the Saatchi Collection," Royal Academy of Arts, London, United Kingdom

"Spank the Monkey," Baltic Centre for Contemporary Art, Gateshead, United Kingdom

"Since 2000: Printmaking Now," Museum of Modern Art, New York, NY

"The Garden Party," Deitch Projects, New York, NY

2005
"Greater New York 2005," MoMA PS1, New York, NY

2004
"Will Boys Be Boys? Questioning Adolescent Masculinity in Contemporary Art" (organized by Independent Curators International and curated by Shamim Momin), Indianapolis Museum of Art, Indianapolis, IN, traveled to Gulf Coast Museum of Art, Largo, FL; Herbert F. Johnson Museum of Art, Cornell University, Ithaca, NY; Museum of Contemporary Art, Denver, CO, and Salina Art Center, Salina, KS

"The Dreamland Artists Club" (presented by Creative Time), Coney Island, New York, NY

"Beautiful Losers: Contemporary Art and Street Culture" (curated by Aaron Rose and Christian Strike), Yerba Buena Center for the Arts, San Francisco, CA and Contemporary Arts Center, Cincinnati, OH, traveled to La Casa Encendida Museum, Madrid, Spain; Arhus Kunstbygning, Aarhus, Denmark; Muzeum Sztuki, Lodz, Poland; Le Tri Postal, Lille, France; Palazzo dell'Arte, Milan, Italy; USF Contemporary Art Museum, Tampa, FL; Contemporary Museum, Baltimore, MD and Orange County Museum of Art, Newport Beach, CA

"La Collection d'Art Contemporain d'Agnès B.," Les Abattoirs Museum, Toulouse, France

"Earthly Delights" (curated by Lisa Tung), Sandra and David Bakalar Gallery, Massachusetts College of Art, Boston, MA

2003
"A New New York Scene," Galerie du Jour, Paris, France

"Lead Poisoning," New Image Art, Los Angeles, CA

"North Star Video Screening," Mori Art Museum, Tokyo, Japan

2002
"SK8 on The Wall," Gallery Rocket, Tokyo, Japan

"Session The Bowl," Deitch Projects, New York, NY

2001
"Spunky," Exit Art, New York, NY

2000
"Critic as Grist" (curated by Michael Portnoy), White Box, New York, NY

"Insights: Interior Spaces in Contemporary Art," Whitney Museum of American Art at Champion, Stamford, CT

SELECT COLLECTIONS

Albright-Knox Art Gallery, Buffalo, NY
AkzoNobel Art Foundation, Amsterdam, Netherlands
Amorepacific Museum of Art, Seoul, Korea
Bank of America, New York, NY
Charles Saatchi Collection, London, United Kingdom
Cincinnati Art Museum, Cincinnati, OH
Cora Diamond Corporation, New York, NY
Cranbrook Art Museum, Bloomfield Hills, MI
Gilberto and Rosa Sandretto Collection, Milan, Italy
Hallmark Art Collection, Kansas City, MO
JPMorgan Chase Art Collection, New York, NY
Malingue Collection, Paris, France
Matthew and Iris Strauss Family Foundation, San Diego, CA
Metropolitan Museum of Art, New York, NY
Michael Krichman and Carmen Cuenca Collection, San Diego, CA
MTV Networks, New York, NY
Museum of Modern Art, New York, NY
Museum of Contemporary Art San Diego, San Diego, CA
Museo de Arte Contemporáneo de Castilla y León, León, Spain
Neuberger Berman Collection, New York, NY
New York Public Library, New York, NY
Orrick, Herrington & Sutcliffe, San Francisco, CA
Peter Norton Family Foundation, Santa Monica, CA
Phillip Schrager Collection of Contemporary Art, Omaha, NE
Pizzuti Collection, Columbus, OH
Richard E. Jacobs Group Collection, Westlake, OH
Saastamoinen Foundation, EMMA – Espoo Museum of Modern Art, Espoo, Finland
Schwab Family Collection, San Francisco, CA
Taguchi Art Collection, Tokyo, Japan
UBS Art Collection, New York, NY
Virginia Museum of Fine Arts, Richmond, VA

Published on the occasion of the exhibition

RYAN McGINNESS
MINDSCAPES

2 April – 9 May 2020

Miles McEnery Gallery
520 West 21st Street
New York NY 10011

tel +1 212 445 0051
www.milesmcenery.com

Director of Publications
Anastasija Jevtovic, New York, NY

Photography by
Farzad Owrang, New York, NY

Color separations by
Echelon, Santa Monica, CA

Catalogue layout by
McCall Associates, New York, NY

Ryan McGinness Studios, Inc.:
Gina Kim, Brendan McGovern
Julia Brodatska, Björk Clarke
Dana Robinson, Jordan Greenblatt

ISBN: 978-1-949327-27-4

Front Cover: *Mindscape 57* (detail), 2019,
acrylic and metal leaf on linen

Back Cover: *Mindscape 31* (detail), 2019,
acrylic and metal leaf on linen

Many of the pigments used in the paintings reproduced in this book reflect different sections of the light spectrum based on their physical properties. These unique attributes are further amplified with the artist's layering techniques. Therefore, in-person observation of the artworks is required for full appreciation. While it is obviously next to impossible to achieve by machine offset printing in four process inks the exact effects of these paints, the greatest possible care was taken to prevent loss of value and detail.